BIOGRAPHIES

Dr. B.R. AMBEDKAR

THE SCULPTOR OF THE INDIAN CONSTITUTION

Manasvi Vohra

V&S PUBLISHERS

Published by:

V&S PUBLISHERS

F-2/16, Ansari Road, Daryaganj, New Delhi - 110002
☎ 23240026, 23240027 • *Fax:* 011-23240028
✉ info@vspublishers.com • 🌐 www.vspublishers.com

Online Brand Store: amazon.in/vspublishers

Regional Office: Hyderabad

5-1-707/1, Brij Bhawan (Beside Central Bank of India Lane)
Bank Street, Koti, Hyderabad - 500 095
☎ 040-24737290
✉ vspublishershyd@gmail.com

Follow us on:   

BUY OUR BOOKS FROM: AMAZON FLIPKART

© Copyright: V&S PUBLISHERS
ISBN 978-81-978303-3-4
New Edition

DISCLAIMER

While every attempt has been made to provide accurate and timely information in this book, neither the author nor the publisher assumes any responsibility for errors, unintended omissions or commissions detected therein. The author and publisher make no representation or warranty with respect to the comprehensiveness or completeness of the contents provided.

All matters included have been simplified under professional guidance for general information only without any warranty for applicability on an individual. Any mention of an organization or a website in the book by way of citation or as a source of additional information doesn't imply the endorsement of the content either by the author or the publisher. It is possible that websites cited may have changed or removed between the time of editing and publishing the book.

Results from using the expert opinion in this book will be totally dependent on individual circumstances and factors beyond the control of the author and the publisher.

It makes sense to elicit advice from well informed sources before implementing the ideas given in the book. The reader assumes full responsibility for the consequences arising out from reading this book.

For proper guidance, it is advisable to read the book under the watchful eyes of parents/guardian. The purchaser of this book assumes all responsibility for the use of given materials and information.

The copyright of the entire content of this book rests with the author/publisher. Any infringement/ transmission of the cover design, text or illustrations, in any form, by any means, by any entity will invite legal action and be responsible for consequences thereon.

Publisher's Note

Since the beginning of our operations in 2010, **V&S Publishers** has been devoted to bringing you one of the best and widest selections of books from across reading genres. Our work is defined by our very name, Value and Substance (V&S), which is at the heart of the books we publish. In becoming one of the leading publishers of general trade books in the mass-appeal genre in India, we have focused on developing a repertoire of titles that not just seek to inspire our readers to grow and flourish in life, but also spark a love for varied cultures and languages. Today, our catalogue has expanded to more than 1000 titles, across the categories of academic, children's stories, parenting, popular science, religion and spirituality, self-improvement, and many more.

Bhimrao Ramji Ambedkar, the father of the constitution of largest democracy, was a man of vision and perseverance. Born in a scheduled caste, he witnessed sheer discrimination in a class based discriminatory Hindu society. He decided to stand against and dedicated his life for the upliftment of the oppressed. He became a lawyer, establish many organizations for the cause, battled in a legal way for the reforms and steered the drafting of the constitution. He faced many challenges from his contemporaries like Gandhi when he demanded reservation for the lower caste.

This biography of BABA SAHEB delves deep into the personal and political dimensions of his life encompassing the discrimination he faced all his life being a Dalit Hindu to the point where he chose to convert to Buddhism.

His life and legacy continues to inspire generations and guide bureaucrats while making policies for the masses.

We sincerely hope our effort in bringing out this offering will be greeted by the warm and enthusiastic reception of our readers.

Contents

Childhood and Early Life

Dr. Bhimrao Ambedkar was born on 14th April in 1891 in the cantonment town of Mhow – formally known as Dr. Ambedkar Nagar in the present day in Madhya Pradesh, to Bhimabai and Ramji Ambadvekar. He was the fourteenth and the last child of Ramji Maloji Sakpal and Bhimabai. Here, it is worth mentioning that there is an interesting anecdote associated with the birth of Ambedkar.

Dr. Ambedkar's place of birth at Mhow, Madhya Pradesh

The story goes that there was an uncle of Ramji Sakpal who had renounced his worldly possessions and had become an ascetic. One day in Mhow, a relative of Ramji Sakpal caught the sight of him while on the way to the river for washing. Upon being informed about his uncle, Ramji rushed out to meet his uncle. It was during this meeting that Ramji's uncle bestowed a boon on him that a son will be born in his family and that he shall, create history one day. Soon after, Ambedkar – a babbling infant who would one day go on to serve as the Chairman of the Drafting Committee of the Constitution of India was born.

Family Roots

Ambedkar was born in the Dalit Mahar caste, a community that was ill treated as untouchables and subjected to socio-economic discrimination. His family held a position of consequence in their ancestral village, Ambavade, which is located near Mandangad, in the Ratnagiri district. His family held a prestigious position of keeping the palanquin that was used to carry the village goddess. Ambedkar's grandfather was a retired military man and one of local repute. He had several children, of which only Ramji Sakpal and his sister, Mira, survived to adulthood.

It is interesting to note that Ambedkar's family practised the Bhakti school of thought, which, was influenced by the teachings of the 15th century poet saint Kabir Das. Characterised by benevolence, compassion, and submission to God, this school of thought, taught its followers to reject the caste system and follow the footsteps of Kabir. As a result, the followers of the Bhakti school believed that anyone who prayed to God belonged to Him, irrespective of their caste.

The Bhakti school of thought also had a huge influence over Ambedkar's mother, Bhimabai and her family. She belonged to the Murbadkar caste, which was considered as untouchable. Bhimabai came from a rich, well-to-do family settled in Murbad village, which is today located in the Thane district of Maharashtra. Her father and uncles served as Subedhar-Majors in the army. The Bhakti school of thought also had a huge influence over Ambedkar's mother, Bhimabai and her family. They were ardent followers of Bhakti philosophy and often engaged in debate and discussion over its ideals and principles.

Early Years

When Ambedkar was two years old, his father had retired from the army. The family then moved to Dapoli in the Konkan region. By the time Ambedkar turned five, he was admitted to a local school where he began his primary education. His father soon moved to Satara where he had landed a job.

Soon after moving to Satara, a tragedy befell the family with the death of Bhimabai. Ambedkar was left motherless at the tender age of six. At this time, the couple had five surviving children out of their 14 kids. These were Balram (the eldest son), Anandrao, Manjula, Tulsi, and Bhimrao, who was the youngest among his siblings. After Bhimabai's death, Ramji Sakpal's sister, Mira, moved in with the family to take care of the children. As time passed, young Bhim quickly became his aunt's favourite.

From Ambavadekar to Ambedkar
The original surname of Ambedkar was 'Ambavadekar', derived from the name of his ancestral village, Ambavade, in the Ratnagiri district. However, out of great affection for young Bhim, his teacher, Mahadev Ambedkar, changed his surname from 'Ambavadekar' to 'Ambedkar' in the school records.

Ambedkar experienced his first brushes with caste discrimination when he started attending school. He, along with other students, who belonged to the lower castes, were segregated from the students who belonged to upper castes. They were treated as untouchables and made to sit separately. In his later writings, Ambedkar described that they were not allowed to touch the vessel containing water, and that a person from a higher caste would pour out water to drink for them from a height. So, on the days when the school peon was not available, they would go without water the whole day. They also did not receive much attention from their teachers owing to their caste.

The Role of Ramji Sakpal

Ramji Sakpal brought up his children with great diligence, ensuring that each of them was firmly grounded in religious life. The family's routine usually began with him singing spiritual hymns in the morning, accompanied by the children, and then again in the evening. He also recited the *Ramayana* and *Mahabharata* to his children every day to inculcate spiritual values in them. He was a strict disciplinarian who made sure the children went to bed early every day and devoted sufficient time to their studies. Ramji Sakpal taught his children Marathi and helped them with English and Arithmetic.

For as many as 14 years, Ramji Sakpal worked as a headmaster in a military school. He was promoted to the rank of a Subedhar-Major in the 2nd Grenadiers. However, when the government prohibited the recruitment of Mahars in the army in 1892, he participated in a protest against the order. He also went on to assist in the drafting of a petition to the government; to withdraw the order. The humanitarian work of Ramji Sakpal and his selfless approach towards working for the betterment of society sowed the seeds of revolutionary ideas that would inspire young Bhim to walk a path of truth, equity, and justice in life.

2

Education and Career

While in Satara, young Bhim started going to high school with his elder brother. However, it was during his school-going years that he experienced the stigma associated with untouchability at close quarters. Countless incidents left Ambedkar disappointed at the lack of social justice and the inability of untouchables to progress in society. Time and again, he suffered discrimination not just at the hands of his classmates and teachers, but also people from day-to-day life that all shaped his personality through adolescence and early adulthood.

As a child, Ambedkar was inventive and unafraid to speak his mind. There are many anecdotes from his childhood that shine light on his fearless attitude of meeting challenges. Right from a young age, he showed a defiant attitude towards those who dictated norms of conduct and behaviour. In one such instance, a barber refused to cut his hair claiming that cutting Bhim's hair would make his razor impure owing to him being an untouchable – and that he would rather shave a buffalo. Such experiences left an indelible mark on the child's mind about the harsh reality of the Indian caste system.

Life Takes a Turn

However, it is interesting to note that young Bhim didn't make great progress in school. To the contrary, he spent more time indulging in his hobbies, notably gardening, and spent all his savings on buying plants. During this phase of his life, Ambedkar also went through emotional turmoil as his father decided to get married for the second time. Ambedkar did not like this new development and wanted to live independently by earning his own livelihood. This thought brought a tide of changes in young Bhim's life, he finally decided to focus on studies, improve his grades and secure a livelihood for himself.

<table>
<tr><td>Stealing Money</td></tr>
<tr><td>Young Bhim was so desperate to go to Bombay to earn a living that he even tried to steal money from his aunt's purse multiple times. Upon realising the gravity of stealing as an offence, he felt ashamed of himself and vowed to study hard to graduate his exams fast, so that he could find a job to support himself.</td></tr>
</table>

Soon, Ramji Sakpal moved his family to Bombay. Here, they started living in Dabak Chawl at Lower Parel. Ambedkar started attending Maratha High School in the city. By this time, Ambedkar had grown proficient in English, owing to the translation exercises. Just like other politicians and scholars of the time, Ambedkar devoted most of his time to reading books and building an expansive repertoire of knowledge.

Remarkable improvement in grades stood as testament to young Bhim's sharp intellect and his dedication to studies. The journey of Ambedkar in the world of knowledge and learning – which would later become his weapons in the fight against untouchability for social justice – kickstarted with his time at Elphinstone High School in 1897. During this time, Ambedkar would sometimes carry tiffin boxes to his relatives who would be working in the mills. He would spend time observing the hard life of the working class at these mills. In his free time, he would play football and cricket with his friends.

Wedding Bells Come Ringing

In 1907, Ambedkar completed his matriculation by scoring grades that were uncommon for those from his community. This achievement called for a celebration among friends and family. News of Bhim's achievement travelled far and wide –

a meeting was organised in Bombay, where famous reformers SK Bhonsle and Krishnaji Arjun Keluskar were present. Keluskar, especially, took great interest in Bhim and admired him for his intelligence. He even encouraged Ramji Sakpal to send Bhim to the university for higher studies.

In the late 19th century, it was common practice for boys to settle into domestic life after achieving good grades in examination. Thus, Ramji Sakpal started looking for a bride for young Bhim. In 1907, Ambedkar was married to a nine-year-old girl, named Rami. Ambedkar was only 16–17 years old then. Later renamed Ramabai, she was a simple, sober girl who came from a humble family; her father, Bhiku Walangkar, worked as a porter in Dapoli.

Ramabai Ambedkar: Wife of B.R. Ambedkar

New Horizons

The same year Ambedkar joined the prestigious Elphinstone College in Bombay. For a while, things seemed to have settled for Ambedkar and his family but problems soon came to the fore. Ambedkar lost a year in college due to ill health; however, a bigger problem arrived when Ramji Sakpal ran out of money to fund Bhim's education.

This was when Keluskar came to his rescue – he requested the Maharaja of Baroda, Sayajirao Gaikwad, to keep his word at an earlier meeting to help a worthy untouchable. Upon meeting Bhim, Sayaji Gaikwad was impressed with the young boy's answers to his questions, and thereafter, a sum of 25 rupees per mensem was assured as a scholarship. Ambedkar was relieved and so was his family.

In 1912, Ambedkar was awarded his degree in Economics and Political Science at the Bombay University. After his graduation from Elphinstone College, he decided to take up the position of a lieutenant with the Baroda State Forces, despite his father's disapproval. Hardly 15 days into the job, he received a telegram that his father was ailing in Bombay. Ambedkar rushed back to the city to look up his father and was heartbroken to see him sinking. Ramji Sakpal passed away soon after his son's arrival on 2nd February in 1913.

A Step Forward Towards Destiny
A twist of fate in the month of June, in 1913, catapulted Ambedkar several steps ahead in his academic journey. The Maharaja of Baroda decided to announce a scholarship scheme for a selection of students to be sent for advanced studies to Columbia University, in the United States. Ambedkar decided to request a meeting with the Maharaja to narrate his ordeal. On 4th June, he signed an agreement to dedicate time to studying certain subjects and serve the state of Baroda for 10 years after graduating his academic programme.

Ambedkar arrived in New York in July the same year. He switched a few residences before settling in the Livingstone Hall Dormitory. Here, he got introduced to Naval Bhathena, a Parsi student, who went on to share a lifelong friendship with Ambedkar. America opened doors of new perspective for Ambedkar – he could finally eat his meals at the same table with his friends and colleagues; eat at regular hours with regular cutlery; and walk around as a free man in its true sense.

Dr. Ambedkar during his higher education years

Ambedkar and his Frugal Ways

Ambedkar was so frugal with his expenses at the Columbia University that he had only two muffins, a piece of meat, or a fish dish along with his cup of coffee every day, despite a large appetite. He did this so that he could send money back to his family in India from his monthly stipend.

Ambedkar spent as many as 18 hours every day for months to earn his M.A. degree in June in 1915. He graduated his exams, majoring in Economics, along with Philosophy, History, Anthropology, and Sociology. At this stage, he wrote his thesis *Ancient Indian Commerce*. During this time, one of Ambedkar's notable early achievements was *Castes in India: Their Mechanism, Genesis and Development* at a seminar conducted by renowned anthropologist, Alexander Goldenweiser.

Encouraged and supported by his continuous academic success, Ambedkar produced his second thesis *National Dividend of India – A Historic and Analytical Study* in 1916. Eight years down the line, his thesis was published as a book titled, *The Evolution of Provincial Finance in British India.*

Ambedkar dedicated this book to The Maharaja of Baroda, Shri Sayajirao Gaekwad, as a token of appreciation for His Highness's efforts in enabling his education.

Dr. Ambedkar pursuing higher education at Columbia University

Success Onwards and Upwards

After meeting success on his career front at Columbia University, Ambedkar set his eyes on London, which was regarded as a prestigious centre of learning across the world. However, towards this end, Ambedkar had to persuade the Maharaja of Baroda to allow him to pursue further studies in London. When he agreed, Ambedkar admitted himself to the Bar course at Gray's Inn in October, in 1916. Simultaneously, he enrolled at the London School of Economics (LSE) where he began work on his doctoral thesis. Owing to his unparalleled ability in Economics, he was allowed to prepare for the D.Sc. by the professors at LSE.

However, in 1917, Ambedkar suffered a setback when his scholarship from Baroda ended. He returned to India, but luck smiled on him when a recommendation from Professor Edwin Cannan allowed him to return to London, to finish his studies after four years. In 1920, Ambedkar returned to London to resume his studies in Economics at the LSE. Due to limited resources, Ambedkar led a life of frugality in London. He spent most part of his day at the London Museum and the London University Library, always engrossed in his books, making the most of each passing day.

Luggage Lost in the Sea

In June 1917, Ambedkar set sail aboard the SS *Kaiser-i-Hind* to travel back to Bombay. His luggage, which mostly consisted of his books, was sent on a different ship. However, this ship was sunk by a German submarine given the war situation. Although he received compensation for the damages, he was heartbroken to lose his valuable collection of books from New York and London.

In 1921, Ambedkar earned the degree of Master of Science for his thesis, *Provincial Decentralization of Imperial Finance in British India*. However, it was in 1922 that he wrote his landmark doctoral thesis, *The Problem of the Rupee*, which was submitted for review to the University of London. The thesis initially ran into troubled waters with the British Imperialist examiners who asked Ambedkar to rewrite much of the thesis without changing the conclusion. By then Ambedkar had to move back to Bombay as his financial resources had nearly dried up. In 1923, he resubmitted the revised version of his thesis from Bombay. It was accepted by the examiners and Ambedkar was finally awarded his Doctoral of Science. Additionally, Ambedkar was called to Bar by Gray's Inn the same year.

Ambedkar's doctoral thesis *The Problem of the Rupee* was published as book in 1923. He dedicated the book to his parents, as a token of respect, for the sacrifices they made to support his education. These events set the stage for Ambedkar to storm into Indian politics, as a barrister armed with academic success from some of the most prestigious institutions in the world – a rare feat achieved by what Indian society labelled an untouchable back then.

3

Crusade Against Untouchability

In 1923, Ambedkar started practising law as a means to work towards emancipation of the untouchables. Towards this end, he even borrowed money from his friend, Naval Bathena, in order to secure a *sanad* (a letter that has the same authority as an edict or decree in India) to practise as a lawyer. By June, the same year, he was able to begin his practice as a barrister. However, the road to establishing himself as a lawyer was rather difficult, owing to his caste, complexion, inexperience in the practice of law, and the hostile demeanour of the people at the Courts. As was with Ambedkar, these difficulties made his resolve to work for the upliftment of untouchables only stronger.

Even before Ambedkar decided to practice law, he tried various other professions in order to support his family. From working as a private tutor and an account to starting an investment consulting, Ambedkar could not keep up any of these lines of work, due to his status of being an untouchable.

Biggest Private Library

Ambedkar once held the distinction of owning the largest private library in the world. Known as *Rajgirh*, his private library at home stocked more than 50,000 books!

One could argue that Ambedkar perhaps suffered worse forms of discrimination along caste lines in academic institutions in India. In 1918, he joined Sydenham College of Commerce and Economics, Bombay, after being selected for professorship. Although the students at the college – who were mostly higher caste Hindus – did not pay much attention to him initially, they soon changed their mind as a result of his refined disposition, deep knowledge and insights on the subject of Economics. Ambedkar soon gained popularity among the students – yet this development didn't stop some of the Gujarati professors to express their objection at him drinking water from the common pot meant for rest of the staff.

Sydenham College of Commerce and Economics

Waiting for a Visa

Written by Ambedkar, *Waiting for a Visa* is now a textbook at Columbia University. In addition, Columbia University compiled a list of the world's top 100 scholars in 2004. Ambedkar was featured in the first position on this list.

First Steps Towards Making his Voice Heard

While Ambedkar was working as a professor at Sydenham, he started establishing communication with untouchables to feel the pulse on the ground. Opportunity came knocking on Ambedkar's door when he was sought to express his opinion on the Depressed Classes (a collective term used for *harijans*, outcastes, pariahs, and untouchables) before the Southborough Committee, which was drafting the Government of India Act, 1919. Ambedkar did not shy away from making the most of this opportunity by calling for the creation of separate electorate and reservation of seats for people from the Depressed Classes in proportion to their overall population.

Next, Ambedkar started a fortnightly paper, known as *Mooknayak* (Leader of the Dumb), on 31st January, in 1920. The Maharaja of Kolhapur, Dattoba Powar, helped him with the initial expenses for establishing the newspaper operations. In the first few editions of the paper, he wrote that it was lamentable that the Hindu society awarded monopoly over knowledge and learning to Brahmins. He drew a link between the lack of education and awareness among the non-Brahmins with higher levels of backwardness. Hence, in Ambedkar's opinion, there was a need to awaken these communities to where they were lacking in order to emancipate them from poverty, illiteracy, and slavery.

Shifts in the Political Climate

The political climate had begun to significantly shift in the following years. Ambedkar's fight against untouchability came against a background of despondency on the part of the extant political parties. He understood that for any major change to arrive in favour of the Depressed Classes would mean breaking free of the patronage offered by high caste Hindu social reformers these communities had grown so accustomed to. He felt there was a need for these oppressed classes to develop a conscience that would inspire them to fight for their elevation in society. He coined the slogan, "Tell the slave he is a slave and he will revolt", towards this end and promoted "self-help", "self-elevation", and "self-respect" as the three essential elements for the upliftment of these communities.

Then came a landmark day on 4th January, in 1925, when Ambedkar founded the Bahishkrit Hitakarini Sabha to enable the socio-economic upliftment of students from Depressed Classes by instilling a love for learning and social service in them. The Sabha also provided guidance to the students to start their own monthly magazine, called *Saraswati Vilas*. In addition, a reading room was opened in Bombay and a Mahar Hockey Club was started to provide healthy means of recreation to these communities, instead of engaging in vices, such as gambling and consuming alcohol.

Logo of Bahishkrit Hitkarni Sabha founded by Dr. B.R. Ambedkar

In 1926, there was yet another breakthrough moment in Ambedkar's quest for self-elevation for his community. Ambedkar had become a prominent lawyer by then. The same year he was approached by three non-Brahmin leaders KK Bagde, Dinkarrao Javalkar, and Kesharao Jedhe, who were charged for publishing a pamphlet that said Brahmins had ruined India by some Brahmins in Pune. Ambedkar's defence in the Sessions Court sealed victory in his favour and his eloquent argument won him acclaim in society in October, in 1926.

<table>
<tr><td>Death of Rajratna</td></tr>
<tr><td>In July 1926, Ambedkar and his wife, Ramabai, lost their son, Rajratna. He was so overcome with grief that he wouldn't part with the dead body of his son. Rajratna's passing came soon after the death of their daughter, Indu, who passed away at infancy.</td></tr>
</table>

Creating Real Impact on the Ground

An acclaimed lawyer; editor of periodicals; and a social reformer, Ambedkar was fast spiralling into the world of politics. In 1925, he was selected to work with the Bombay Presidency Committee, which would in turn work with the Simon Commission – an all-European body. The commission was met with widespread protest across the country. Notwithstanding this, Ambedkar wrote a set of recommendations for the Constitution of India, as it would stand in the future.

By 1927, Ambedkar set a stage for galvanising the members of the Depressed Classes to take action towards improving the political and socio-economic life of untouchables. A conference was called at Mahad by the Kolaba District Depressed Classes from 19th to 20th March, in 1927. Ambedkar was invited to the event, which was attended by around 10,000 leaders, workers of these oppressed communities from all over Maharashtra and Gujarat.

It was decided at this conference that the attendees would march to Chowdar Tank to take water as a symbol of asserting their right to take water from a public source. The tank was used by Hindus, Muslims, and Christians; however, untouchables were barred from taking water from there. After marching peacefully to the tank, Ambedkar was the first to take water from the tank and drink it. Scores of attendees followed suit and drank water from the tank. This moment in history gave faith and belief to the Depressed Classes that unity of thought and action could go a long way in bringing about real impact on the ground.

This incident was, of course, reaped widespread criticism towards Ambedkar and his ideas. In order to counter this with structured opinion, he started a fortnightly Marathi newspaper, *Bahishkrit Bharat*, on 3rd April, in 1927, in Bombay. Ambedkar went on to leverage the newspaper to drive home the point that the need of the hour was to secure political representation of the Depressed Classes by means of upcoming political reforms, or else these communities would never advance socially or economically. Real change, according to Ambedkar, would begin with the untouchables gaining access to public resources and temples.

Logo of Bahishkrit Bharat: Fortnightly started by B.R. Ambedkar

In context of education, Ambedkar was also of the firm opinion that in order to bring the depressed classes "… to the level of equality, then the only remedy is to adopt the principle of inequality and to give favoured treatment to those who are below the level." These thoughts laid the future ground for affirmative action for students belonging to oppressed castes.

Ambedkar also raised the issue of the academia dominated by the Brahmin community who nursed a disdain for the Depressed Classes. According to Ambedkar, the act of treating education as a domain reserved for a certain caste or class was against the very essence of education, which was to bring enlightenment to the mind.

Laying Ground for Progress Ahead

Later, on 25th December, in 1927, at a Conference, Ambedkar bravely rejected the sublime authority of certain ancient as well as contemporary Hindu scriptures, which preached social inequality. Notable among these was the *Manusmriti* – written by the ancient law-maker Manu – that was deeply criticised by Ambedkar and other conference attendees for justifying social, political, and economic cruelty and injustice against the Depressed Classes at the hands of the upper castes.

It was at this event that a pyre was lit and Ambedkar, accompanied by fellow leaders and Conference attendees, set copies of the *Manusmriti* on fire. It was a historic act of outrightly rejecting the age-old conventions that had restricted the growth and damaged self-respect of the Depressed Classes for centuries. Over the years, 25th December came to be celebrated as *Manusmriti* Burning Day by Dalits and followers of Ambedkar.

From 1927 to 1929, Ambedkar and other leaders of the Depressed Classes did much to push for reforms to recognise the rights of these classes, including the right to enter a place of worship. These three years were crucial for the lead-up to the Satyagraha that was to take place in 1930, just a few days before Mahatma Gandhi was to launch his Dandi March. A Satyagraha Committee had been formed in Nashik by the Depressed Classes to prepare for this big event: a call to the oppressed communities to assert their right to enter the

Kalaram Temple, which was dedicated to Lord Rama. As many as 15,000 volunteers marched towards the temple, under the presidentship of Ambedkar, with the objective of entering the temple premises. However, upon reaching the venue, the gates of the temple were closed not just to the Satyagrahis, but also for Hindus.

However, the Satyagraha continued in the face of the struggle. A few days later, the Satyagrahis congregated near the temple to see the chariot procession. But all hell broke lose as rioters ran amok in the crowd, resulting in police firing, stone pelting, and loss of life and property. The Kalaram Temple remained closed for an entire year in the wake of this unrest. Despite the criticism that came Ambedkar's way, a statement had been made, the stage had been set, their voice had been heard. It was clear from this event that the Depressed Classes were not going to give up their fight to assert their rights.

4

Political Career

Over the years, Ambedkar had emerged as a fiery hero for the oppressed classes through his relentless struggle to uplift their political and socio-economic condition. He had made significant efforts to dismantle the repressive system through symbolic yet powerful gestures of leading the march to Chowdar Tank to drink water from a public source and to Kalaram Temple to enable his community to get access to a public place of worship. It can be said that at this point, Ambedkar was seen as a torch bearer of justice, social equity, hope, and strength among the Depressed Classes.

A Satyagraha for Water

Babasaheb was the world's first and only Satyagrahi who led a demonstration for access to clean water.

Poona Pact

A turning point was to arrive in Ambedkar's political career in 1932. The British Colonial government declared the introduction of a separate electorate for Depressed Classes in the Communal Award in 1932. To put it simply, the Award was to grant separate seats to the Depressed Classes in the Provincial Assemblies, as well as the right to exercise a double vote. This meant that they could not only elect their own representatives, but also vote in the general constituencies.

The Communal Award was met with widespread protest, notably by Mahatma Gandhi who feared that a separate electorate for the Depressed Classes would further fragment the Hindu community. The Award was seen as a way to break down the country politically by giving separate electorates to Muslims, Christians, Sikhs, and Europeans. Following this announcement, Mahatma Gandhi declared his pledge of fast unto death while being imprisoned in Yerwada Central Jail, in Poona, to prevent the separation of the untouchable Hindus from the caste Hindus. This created friction between Ambedkar and Gandhi, as the former stayed firm on his decision, saying:

"So far as I am concerned, I am willing to consider everything, though I am not willing to allow the right of the Depressed Classes to be curtailed in any way. ..."

Ambedkar's steadfast approach had criticism, appreciation, threats, as well as support from different factions of society. However, one thing was clear – Ambedkar's dedication to the cause of untouchables had opened the eyes of society at large, as well as the Press and the patriots, to do something for the betterment of these oppressed communities.

With both Gandhi and Ambedkar holding onto their personal views on the matter of separate electorates, prominent congressional party members and activists, notably Madan Mohan Malaviya and Palwankar Baloo, requested Ambedkar to meet Mahatma Gandhi at Yerwada. Negotiations followed between the leaders to settle the total number of seats in the provincial assembles, duration of reserved seats, and how the seats should be distributed.

Then, finally, on 25th September, in 1932, the historical Poona Pact was signed between Ambedkar – on behalf of the Depressed Classes – and Madan Mohan Malaviya – on behalf of the rest of Hindus. The pact awarded reserved seats to the Depressed Classes in Provincial Assemblies within the general electorate. Hence, it provided for the formation of single, unified electorate, with primary and secondary elections allowing the untouchables to select candidates as per their preference.

Dr. Ambedkar with other political leaders after signing the Poona Pact with Mahatama Gandhi

A Radical Move

Following the events of the preceding years, Ambedkar had come to the conclusion that in order to achieve change on the ground level, it was necessary to gain political power. This prompted him to change the course of his movement to inspiring his followers to gear themselves towards achieving political gains and develop their strength towards achieving material advancement.

In 1935, the Government Law College, in Bombay, appointed Ambedkar as its Principal. Ambedkar served as the Principal of the college for two years, while closely following the developments on the political front. However, tragedy struck him when his wife, Ramabai, who had been ailing for a long time breathed her last on 27th May, in 1935. Ambedkar was inconsolable and went into mourning for some time.

Dr. Ambedkar with his colleagues at the Government Law College Bombay in 1928

Later that year, in October, a political storm was stirred at the Yeola Conference in Nasik, where Ambedkar announced that he wanted to change his religion from Hinduism to Buddhism. Since all other movements had failed to enable the untouchables to assert their rights in society, Ambedkar was gradually coming to the conclusion that the only way an untouchable could live a life of dignity was by converting to another religion. Reflecting on the discrimination he had endured all his life owing to being born an untouchable Hindu, he famously said, "I solemnly assure you that I will not die a Hindu."

A Man of Exceptional Ability

Ambedkar was an expert in 64 subjects. He was proficient in 9 languages: Hindi, Pali, Sanskrit, English, French, German, Marathi, Persian, and Gujarati. Besides that, he spent about 21 years studying all of the world's faiths in comparative detail.

The conference was held to take stock of the struggle led by leaders of the Depressed Classes to assert their rights in the last 10 years. It was attended by close to 10,000 members of the oppressed communities. What followed was a stream of communication from the religious leaders of various religions courting Ambedkar to convert to their religion. After all, his steadfast approach towards rights, equality, and social equity would have provided an impetus to their faith as well.

Achieving Change Through Political Power

In August 1936, Ambedkar established a political party called the Independent Labour Party. In 1937, the party contested the Bombay elections to the Central Legislative Assembly. It fought elections for 13 reserved and 4 general seats, of which it won 11 and 3 seats, respectively. The same year, Ambedkar published his landmark book *Annihilation of Caste* that was founded on the thesis he had written in New York. The book was a fierce criticism of the caste system in general and called out the enabling role of orthodox Hindu religious leaders in perpetuating caste-based discrimination. He also protested against the term *Harijan* (a person belonging to God), which was coined by Mahatma Gandhi, to address the untouchables.

Ambedkar also served as the Minister of Labour on the Defence Advisory Committee and the Viceroy's Executive Council. In 1939, on the event of the Day of Deliverance at Bhindi Bazaar, in Bombay, both Ambedkar and Jinnah delivered a fiery address, criticising the Congress party for their policies. Ambedkar famously announced at the event that the Depressed Classes he had worked with were 20 times more repressed owing to Congress party's policies than Indian Muslims.

A Flourishing Career in Writing

From 1941 to 1945, Ambedkar wrote a number of books that went on to be in the news for their highly controversial subject and treatment. Notable among these is *Thoughts on Pakistan*, a critique of the Muslim League's demand to create a separate Muslim state of Pakistan. In the book, Ambedkar analyses the very idea of Pakistan, arguing that Hindus should in fact concede the state to the Muslims. Over the years, scholars have agreed that this landmark book played a vital role in determining the course of action taken by the National Congress and Muslim League, and how it led to the ultimate Partition of India.

With the book *What Congress and Gandhi Have Done to the Untouchables*, Ambedkar continued to launch attacks on Mahatma Gandhi and the Congress for their views on the matter of the Depressed Classes. This was followed by *Who were the Shudras?* in which he tried to explain the origin of the *shudras* (those regarded as the lowest in the caste system) and how they are a different category of people from the untouchables. Ambedkar wrote another scathing book about Hinduism called *The Untouchables: A Thesis on the Origins of Untouchability* in 1948.

Political Wins and Losses

This was also the time when Ambedkar's political party, the Independent Labour Party, was undergoing a transformation in his supervision. The party grew into the All India Scheduled Castes Federation. However, the party fared poorly in the elections for the Constituent Assembly of India in 1946. Notwithstanding the loss of the party, Ambedkar was elected into the Bengal Constituent Assembly, with the Muslim League helming the wheel.

A Great Visionary
Ambedkar had recommended a division of Madhya Pradesh and Bihar to ensure better and holistic development of the states way back in the 1950s. However, this recommendation was implemented after 50 years in the year 2000 when Chhattisgarh was carved out of Madhya Pradesh and Jharkhand out of Bihar.

In 1952, Ambedkar contested the first Indian General Elections from Bombay North. However, he lost to Narayan Kajrolkar, his former assistant who was fielded by the Congress Party then. Despite the defeat, Ambedkar became a Member of the Rajya Sabha the same year. In 1954, Ambedkar tried to contest for a Lok Sabha seat from Bhandara, but he lost yet again.

5

Drafting of Indian Constitution and Buddhism

In April 1947, Ambedkar attended the third session of the Constituent Assembly. This session was of crucial importance as it was during this session that the reports by the Advisory Committee and the Fundamental Rights Committee were adopted by the Constituent Assembly. The day of 29th April marked a landmark moment in the history of India when the Constituent Assembly announced, "Untouchability in any form is abolished and the imposition of any disability on that account shall be an offence." Unfortunately, Ambedkar barely received any recognition from the international press for his struggle through the years that had led to this outcome. Ambedkar's crowning moment was yet to arrive.

Political Recognition

On 15th July 1947, the Act of Indian Independence was passed by the British Parliament. This event made the Constituent Assembly a sovereign body. With the partition of Bengal, many of the members lost their seats in the Constituent Assembly. Luckily for Ambedkar, he was selected by the Bombay Legislative Congress Party to replace Dr. MR Jayakar, who had earlier resigned, in the Constituent Assembly. The wins kept coming from hereon. Soon, Pandit Jawaharlal Nehru asked

Ambedkar if he would be interested in joining the Cabinet of free India as a Minister for Law, to which Ambedkar, of course, agreed. But this was only the beginning of great things to come Ambedkar's way.

The Indian Tri-Colour

Ambedkar is also credited with including the Ashok Chakra in the Indian Tri-colour. The national flag was designed by notable freedom fighter and Gandhian Pingali Venkayya.

Then arrived the greatest day in the history of India's struggle for independence. On 15th August 1947, India was declared a free nation. This was followed by the formation of a Drafting Committee by the Constituent Assembly on 29th August. The Drafting Committee comprised Ambedkar as the Chairman and N Madhava Rao, Syed M Saadullah, Sir Alladi Krishnamachari, and TT Krishnamachari among its members. With this development, Ambedkar hit a career milestone. An untouchable who suffered caste-based discrimination through his life and fiercely fought for the emancipation of the Depressed Classes was now the Father of the Constitution as well as the Minister of Law in New India.

Dr. BR ambedkar along with other members of Drafting committee of the Indian Constitution

Drafting the Constitution of India

At this point, Ambedkar's health was deteriorating. Despite his ill health, Ambedkar was working tirelessly day in and day out to draft the Constitution. As the Chairman of the Committee, his task was to not just provide his input in the drafting of the Constitution, but also defend the draft in the debates that were to follow its presentation. Among the notable sections drafted by Ambedkar, the section on *States and Minorities* is of significance. Ambedkar submitted the section to the Sub-Committee on Fundamental Rights of the Constituent Assembly. A prototype of the Constitution in itself – complete with its own preamble – the section provided for a strong mechanism of constitutional protection to scheduled castes.

Dr. Ambedkar handing final draft of the Indian constitution to Rajendra Prasad

A Lifelong Commitment

Although Ambedkar had resolved to never marry again, his ill health and loneliness of old age prompted him to change his mind. He decided to marry Dr. Sharada Kabir whom he had met during his medical treatment in Bombay. Their marriage was solemnised on 15th April, in 1948, at his residence in Delhi. Dr. Kabir adopted the name Savita Ambedkar after marriage and cared for her husband for the rest of his life.

Ambedkar finished reviewing the draft of the Constitution of India in the last week of February 1948. It was then submitted to the President of the Constituent Assembly, after which it was presented to the country for opinion. The Constitution was formally adopted by the Constituent Assembly on 26th November, in 1949.

Additionally, as the first Minister of Law in India, Ambedkar was working on legal reforms befitting modern India. It is worth mentioning here that the ideas he presented to the Hilton Young Commission served as an inspiration for the formation of the Reserve Bank of India.

The Road to Buddhism

On 2nd January, in 1950, Ambedkar returned to Bombay after his successful run as the Chairman of the Drafting Committee. He was mobbed by prominent personalities and his followers who greeted him with great enthusiasm upon his arrival. On 11th January, he was presented a copy of the Constitution of India in a golden casket at a meeting organised by the Bombay Scheduled Castes Federation, in Parel, in Bombay. Ambedkar declared at this meeting that his objective of being part of the Constituent Assembly was to safeguard the interests of the Scheduled Castes, and not out of political ambition.

However, as the years went by, Ambedkar grew increasingly vocal about his views on Hinduism. He attacked Hindu godmen and spoke critically about the social gospel of Hinduism that he felt was grounded in inequality. By contrast, he opined that Buddhism was grounded on the idea of morality or *Dharma*. Although he had not made a steadfast decision on the adoption of Buddhism, the seeds of conversion were sown in Ambedkar's mind.

Ambedkar had earlier thought about converting to Sikhism, which had adopted a combative approach towards oppression in all forms, and thus, appealed ideologically to the leaders of scheduled castes back then. However, Ambedkar changed his mind after successive rounds of discussions with Sikh leaders, when he felt he might be relegated to a "second rate" Sikh status if he indeed converted to Sikhism.

Conversion to Buddhism

In 1950, he travelled to Ceylon (present-day Sri Lanka) to attend a meeting of the World Fellowship of Buddhists. During this visit, he attended a meeting in Colombo, where he urged the Buddhists of Ceylon to accept the Depressed Classes in the country and work towards safeguarding the interests of these oppressed communities. In the later years, while dedicating a Buddhist *vihara* in Pune, Ambedkar finally announced that he would convert to Buddhism after finishing the book he was writing on Buddhism.

This declaration was followed by his successive visits to Burma (present-day Myanmar) to attend the third conference of the World Fellowship of Buddhists. Ambedkar then went on to establish the Bharatiya Bauddha Mahasabha in 1955. He finished writing his book, titled *The Buddha and His Dhamma* in 1956. The book was published posthumously.

Finally, on 14th October, in 1956, the historic day arrived. Over 20 years after Ambedkar had declared his intention to convert to another religion, he organised a formal public ceremony to convert to Buddhism in Nagpur. The ceremony was attended by around 3,65,000 followers of Ambedkar who converted to Buddhism along with their leader. The ceremony was performed in a traditional manner and presided over by Buddhist monks and important figures. At the ceremony, Ambedkar and his wife accepted the Three Refuges and Five Precepts from a Buddhist monk, thereby changing their religion for good.

A Modern-Day Bodhisattva

Ambedkar was conferred the highest Buddhist title of "Bodhisattva" by Buddhist monks at the World Buddhist Conference, in Kathmandu, in 1954. His book, *The Buddha and His Dhamma*, is regarded as a "scripture" by Indian Buddhists.

Here, it is important to understand that Ambedkar's life-changing decision to convert to Buddhism was a result of his informed understanding that the only way for the Depressed Classes to gain equality in society was to denounce the caste system itself. On the day of the conversion, Ambedkar famously said, "… For getting human treatment, convert yourselves. Convert to getting organized. Convert to becoming strong. Convert for securing equality. Convert to getting liberty."

After converting to Buddhism, Ambedkar went to Kathmandu, in Nepal, to attend the Fourth World Buddhist Conference. At this time, he had started work on two books, namely, *The Buddha or Karl Marx* and *Revolution and Counter-Revolution in Ancient India*, both of which remain incomplete, owing to his sudden death on 6th December, in 1956.

Dr. Ambedkar delivering a speech at Fourth World Buddhist Conference

6

Legacy

Ambedkar had long been a patient of diabetes. From June to October in 1954, his medical condition worsened, owing to the side effects of medicines. Ambedkar had just finished his work on his book, *The Buddha and His Dhamma*, when he passed away in his sleep on 6th December, in 1956, at his residence on Alipore Road, in New Delhi. The news of his death spread very fast in the political circle of New Delhi. His wife, Savita Ambedkar, was flooded with calls from the then Prime Minister Pandit Jawaharlal Nehru, Jagjivan Ram, who was the then Minister of Communications and the Deputy Chairman of the Council of States, who paid their tribute to the celebrated leader. Later, Jagjivan Ram also arranged for a plane to fly his body to Bombay.

The funeral procession was led by thousands of his grieving followers from his residence to the Delhi Airport. When the body arrived at Santa Cruz Airport, a silent procession proceeded to Rajagriha, the former home of Ambedkar in Bombay. A pervasive air of grief prevailed over the city as lakhs of people gathered to pay their last homage to Ambedkar, including political party leaders, trade union leaders, scholars, and his followers.

Residence of Babasaheb Ambedkar, Rajgriha

A Buddhist Cremation

On 7th December – the day of Ambedkar's cremation – all factories, railway workshops, docks, and textile mills in the city were declared closed. Processions were carried out in various cities, including Nagpur and Sholapur, in remembrance of Ambedkar. On 7th December, a Buddhist cremation was held at Dadar Chowpatty beach. The event witnessed the attendance of as many as 500,000 mourners. As his funeral pyre was lit by his son, Yashwantrao, at 7:30 pm, the crowd wept at the passing of a great leader who had dedicated his life to the emancipation of the oppressed. In an unprecedented move, the Bombay Police paid their tribute by sounding the last post, which was accorded to a non-official personality for the first time in the city.

Ambedkar left behind his son, Yashwantrao Ambedkar, who died in 1977, and his wife, Savita Ambedkar, who passed away in 2003. After Ambedkar's death, his wife and son carried forward his movement for the socio-economic upliftment of the oppressed classes. The Buddhist Society of India appointed Yashwantrao its 2nd President in 1957. He also served as the member of the Maharashtra Legislative Council from 1960 to 1966. Today, Ambedkar's elder grandson, Prakash Yashwant

Ambedkar, serves as the Chief Advisor to the Buddhist Society of India and heads the Vanchit Bahujan Aghadi. He has also served in both the Houses of the Parliament. His younger grandson, Anandraj Ambedkar, leads the Republican Sena.

Son of Dr. B.R Ambedkar: Yashwantrao Ambedkar

Notable Reactions

The following year, Ambedkar's death continued to be mourned. In the Lok Sabha session, Prime Minister Nehru remarked that the country will forever remember Ambedkar as a "symbol of revolt" for being the voice of the oppressed in Hindu society. Despise his controversial stance on many issues, Ambedkar had fearlessly played the role of providing constructive criticism to the government for its discharge of duties towards the public at large. At the end of his address, Pandit Nehru requested the House to be adjourned for the day, as a mark of respect to the departed soul.

The then President of India, Dr. Rajendra Prasad, expressed that Ambedkar's contribution as the Father of the Indian Constitution was of utmost importance and his lifelong work towards the emancipation of the Depressed Classes could never be overstated.

The former Minister of Home Affairs, C. Rajagopalachari, also expressed his grief over Ambedkar's death, opining that Ambedkar's later act of conversion to Buddhism was more anti-Hindu in nature rather than one of accepting the compassion and morality that the religion stands for. He observed that Ambedkar was an upright man of great jurist sense and erudition.

Legacy After Death

After Ambedkar's untimely passing, an order was passed by the then Chief Minister of Maharashtra, Yashwantrao Chavan, to award 11 acres of land in Nagpur – where the Diksha ceremony was performed on 14th October, in 1956 – to the Buddhist societies to build memorials dedicated to Ambedkar. Following this, a statue was installed at the Old Secretariat, in Bombay, as well as a pagoda was built in Dadar Chowpatty in 1968. On 2nd April, in 1967, a 12-ft-high bronze statue – sculpted by BV Wagh – of Ambedkar was erected in the Parliament complex, in Delhi. The statue was unveiled by the then President of India, Dr. Sarvepalli Radhakrishnan. In addition, a memorial commemorating Ambedkar was founded at his residence in Delhi. On 12th April, in 1990, a grand portrait of Ambedkar, painted by noted artist Zeba Amrohawi, was unveiled by the then Prime Minister, VP Singh, at the Central Hall of the Parliament House. Additionally, the Parliamentary Museum and the Archives section in the Parliament House features a portrait of Ambedkar.

In the years following his death, his family members found numerous unfinished manuscripts and drafts among his notes and papers. These were eventually made public for the knowledge of his followers and scholars. Notable among these is *Waiting for a Visa*, which is regarded as an autobiographical work, and covers the time period from 1935 to 1936.

Public Recognition

In 1990, Ambedkar was awarded the Bharat Ratna, which is the highest civilian honour in India, by the Government of India. Today, there are many public buildings and institutions that are named after Ambedkar in honour of his timeless contribution to our society, notably Ambedkar University in Delhi; Dr. BR Ambedkar National Institute of Technology in Jalandhar, in Punjab; and Dr. Babasaheb Ambedkar International Airport, in Nagpur, in Maharashtra.

In 2015, the Maharashtra Government was finally able to acquire the house in London, in which Ambedkar stayed during his days at the London School of Economics in the 1920s. The house is located on 10 King Henry's Road, in Chalk Farm, in north London. The historic deal cost the Maharashtra Government 3.1 million pounds and was presided over by the Indian High Commission. As of 2020, it was decided by the Indian High Commission that the house will be converted into a museum-and-memorial dedicated to Ambedkar.

Ambedkar's birthday, 14th April, is now observed as Ambedkar Jayanti (or Bhim Jayanti), which has been declared a public holiday. Even to this day, his followers continue to congregate in large numbers at his memorial in Mumbai on his birth and death anniversary, as well as on 14th October, which was later declared Dhamma Chakra Pravartan Din, in Nagpur. Bookshops are set up across the city and followers carry forward his message "Educate, Agitate, and Organise!" all around.

7

Noteworthy Achievements

Dr. Bhimrao Ambedkar has been among the leading socio-political reformers in modern India. His legacy has left an indelible mark on society, with the initiatives he took during his lifelong struggle for social justice and equity. Over the years, his efforts transformed social as well as political sphere through path-breaking reforms, notably in the areas of socio-economic policies and affirmative action, especially in the sector of education.

Ambedkar's stellar reputation as an academician led him to being selected as the first Minister of Law and Justice in independent India. He was also appointed as the Chairman of the Drafting Committee of the Constitution. Simply put, Ambedkar's life served as an inspiration for building a modern, inclusive India. As an economist, a politician, a jurist, and a social reformer, Ambedkar made huge achievements in each of these spheres, of which the significant ones are mentioned here:

1. Ambedkar was the first Indian to complete a doctorate in economics overseas. According to him, India's economy could benefit from industrialisation and agricultural expansion. Ambedkar championed the cause for national economic and social development, emphasising the importance of residential facilities, public health, and education as fundamental amenities.

2. He was the first legislator in the country to introduce a Bill to end agricultural tenant serfdom.

3. Ambedkar founded the Finance Commission of India

in 1951. He established the commission to address the vertical and horizontal fiscal imbalances in the country. Vertical balances refer to the imbalance between the central and state governments owing to disproportionate expenditure incurred by state governments compared to their sources of revenue. Horizontal imbalances refer to the differences among the states as a result of varied historical backgrounds and resources.

4. Ambedkar worked towards the fruition of the Poona Pact that went on to provide fair electoral representation to the Depressed Classes in the legislature during the British Colonial era in 1932.

5. The Reserve Bank of India was established in response to the recommendations of the Hilton Young Commission, which in turn was based on the guidelines presented by Ambedkar in his landmark work, *The Problem of the Rupee: Its Origin and Solution.*

6. He established three political parties: the Independent Labour Party, the Republican Party of India, and the All India Scheduled Caste Federation. All these political parties played an important role in uniting the Depressed Classes and raising awareness of their concerns.

7. Ambedkar's foresight led to the foundation of the Central Water Commission and integrated management of water resources through the creation of river valley projects, such as the Hirakud Dam Project on the Mahanadi and the Damodar River Valley Project.

8. The River Board Act 1956 and the Inter-State Water Dispute Act are both the result of Ambedkar's vision.

9. Ambedkar opposed the introduction of the Industrial Disputes Bill in 1937 in the Bombay Assembly because it eliminated the right of workers to strike.

10. As a member of the labour movement, he promoted "fair conditions of life of labour" rather than establishing "fair conditions of work" and established the framework for the government's labour policy.

11. In a 2012 poll by History TV18 and CNN-IBN, Ambedkar was voted "The Greatest Indian", ahead of Pandit Jawaharlal Nehru and Sardar Patel.

8

Ambedkar's Famous Quotes

Here are a few inspiring quotes by Dr. Bhimrao Ambedkar that reflect his indomitable spirit and dedication towards upliftment of the oppressed class of society:

- "Freedom of mind is the real freedom."

- "A person whose mind is not free though he may not be in chains, is a slave, not a free man."

- "One whose mind is not free, though he may not be in prison, is a prisoner and not a free man."

- "One whose mind is not free though alive, is no better than dead."

- "Freedom of mind is the proof of one's existence."

- "Cultivation of mind should be the ultimate aim of human existence."

- "Nothing is infallible. Nothing is binding forever. Everything is subject to inquiry and examination."

- "I like the religion that teaches liberty, equality and fraternity."

- "If I find the constitution being misused, I shall be the first to burn it."

- "We must stand on our own feet and fight as best as we can for our rights. So carry on your agitation and organize your forces. Power and prestige will come to you through struggle."

- "Indifferentism is the worst kind of disease that can affect people."

- "Humans are mortal. So are ideas. An idea needs propagation as much as a plant needs watering. Otherwise both will wither and die."

- "A great man is different from an eminent one in that he is ready to be the servant of the society."

- "I measure the progress of a community by the degree of progress which women have achieved."

- "Democracy is not merely a form of government. It is primarily a mode of associated living, of conjoint communicated experience. It is essentially an attitude of respect and reverence towards fellow men."

- "Life should be great rather than long."

- "Sincerity is the sum of all moral qualities."

- "If you believe in living a respectable life, you believe in self-help which is the best help."

- "Political tyranny is nothing compared to the social tyranny and a reformer who defies society is a more courageous man than a politician who defies Government."

- "For a successful revolution it is not enough that there is discontent. What is required is a profound and thorough conviction of the justice, necessity and importance of political and social rights."

- "So long as you do not achieve social liberty, whatever freedom is provided by the law is of no avail to you."

9

Learning from Ambedkar's Life

Dr. Ambedkar dedicated his life to championing for human rights for the oppressed sections of society. Ambedkar relentlessly fought to ensure a life of dignity for the Depressed Classes. Born an untouchable and treated as an outcast throughout his childhood and even in his adult life, Ambedkar rose the ranks to become a formidable national personality through sheer dedication, hard work, will power, and resilience.

The man who once carried tiffin boxes to mills as a boy, almost starved himself to save money while studying abroad, and faced widespread political opposition later in life never let his spirit down and continued to charge ahead to create a life of purpose. Given the odds he was up against since his childhood, Ambedkar's rise to becoming an economist, a professor, political leader, lawyer, law-maker, an author, and more importantly, a liberator of the suppressed classes continues to serve as an inspiration to scores of young minds across India.

One of the aspects that distinguishes Ambedkar's life journey from that of many others is that Ambedkar did not come from money or privilege. It was only due to his incisive mind and stellar record in academics that led to his capabilities being recognised at every stage, thereby paving the way for distinctions and scholarships. His knowledge and learning played a vital role throughout his life journey and went on to shape the political climate of the time and even the later years. As Chairperson of the Drafting Committee of the Constitution, he ensured his ideals and principles reflected in the historic document, both in letter and spirit.

Ambedkar's achievements prove that an undying determination to rise above odds can enable a person to conquer all difficulties. His life remains an inspiration to people, and especially the oppressed classes, that irrespective of a person's caste, class, riches, money, or privilege, a person can accomplish his goals through self-discipline, patience, sincerity, and courage.